the *Gift* of **Love**

We **love** *because* **God** *loved us first.*

1 John 4:19 CEV

To _______________________________

____

____

____

From _______________________________

Date _______________________________

 Our Daily Bread Publishing™

the **Gift** *of* **Love**

© 2022 Our Daily Bread Publishing

the **Gift** concept

Developed and designed by 2K/DENMARK

Typeset using the Triptych font family

ISBN 978-1-64070-191-5

Printed in China

Love. It creates the most exhilarating emotional high known
to humanity—the overwhelming fullness of spirit when a child
is born, the heart-pounding anticipation of reuniting with
someone special. And it also has the means to deliver the most
excruciating emotional pain—losses, betrayals, absences.
The more we love, the greater the agony.

But we know that love is so much more than simply emotion.
Love in action, we say. And we don't mean hugs of affection.
We mean service. We mean sharing. We mean sacrifice.
When emotions ebb and flow, love can remain, steady and
strong. What kind of power is that? Where does that come from?

The Bible gives us the answer. The Source. God. God who
loved us first, and loves us still.

Savor these words from God's book, the Bible. Slow down with
them. Let them stir you up, or even trip you up. Let them speak
to you about love in ways you've never heard before. Or maybe
in ways you've heard all your life. Whatever their impact,
in every situation, every second of every day,
remember this one truth:
You are **loved.**

We **love** because **God** **loved** us first.

This is how **God** showed **his** **love** among us: **He** sent **his** one and only **Son** into the world that we might live through **him**.

1 John 4:9 NIV

For unto us
a **Child** is born, ...
Wonderful,
Counselor,
Mighty **God**,
Everlasting **Father**,
Prince of Peace.

Isaiah 9:6 NKJV

For **God** expressed **His** love for the world in this way: **He** gave **His** only **Son** so that whoever believes in **Him** will not face everlasting destruction, but will have everlasting life.

John 3:16 VOICE

This is
how we know
what **love** is:
Jesus Christ
laid down
his life for us.

1 John 3:16 NIV

God shows his **love** for us in that while we were still sinners, **Christ** died for us.

Romans 5:8 ESV

The free gift
of **God**
is eternal life
in **Christ Jesus**
our **Lord.**

Romans 6:23 ESV

Christ will make **his** home
in your hearts
as you trust in **him**.
Your roots will grow down
into **God's** **love**
and keep you strong.
… How wide, how long,
how high, and how deep
his **love** is.

May you experience
the **love** of **Christ**,
though it is too great
to understand fully.
Then you will be
made complete
with all the fullness of life
and power that comes
from **God**.

Because **your** steadfast love is better than life, my lips will praise **you**.

See what great **love** the **Father** has lavished on us, that we should be called children of **God!**

1 John 3:1 NIV

For I am convinced that neither death nor life, neither angels nor demons, neither the present nor the future, nor any powers, neither height nor depth,

nor anything else
in all creation,
will be able to separate
us from the **love** of **God**
that is in **Christ Jesus**
our **Lord.**

Your unfailing **love**,
O **LORD**, is as vast
as the heavens;
your faithfulness reaches
beyond the clouds.
Your righteousness is like
the mighty mountains,
your justice like the
ocean depths.

You care for people and
animals alike, O **LORD**.
How precious is **your**
unfailing **love**, O **God!**
All humanity finds shelter
in the shadow
of **your** wings.

Psalm 36:5–7 NLT

Let all who take refuge
in **you** rejoice;
let them sing
joyful praises forever.
Spread **your** protection
over them,

that all who **love your** name
may be filled with joy.
For **you** bless the godly,
O LORD;
you surround them
with **your** shield
of **love**.

With everlasting **love** I will have compassion on you," says the **LORD**, your **Redeemer**.

Isaiah 54:8 ESV

You,
O Lord,
are a **God**
merciful
and gracious,
slow to anger
and abounding
in steadfast love
and faithfulness.

Psalm 86:15 ESV

o you think anyone is going to be able to drive a wedge between us and **Christ's love** for us? There is no way!

Not trouble,
not hard times,
not hatred,
not hunger,
not homelessness,
not bullying threats,
not backstabbing,
not even the worst sins
listed in Scripture.

Romans 8:35 MSG

Jesus spoke: ...
"**I** give you a new command:
Love each other deeply and fully. Remember the ways that **I** have **loved** you, and demonstrate your **love** for others in those same ways."

John 13:31, 34 VOICE

This is the kind of **love** we are talking about—not that we once upon a time **loved** God, but that **he loved** us and sent **his Son** as a sacrifice to clear away our sins and the damage they've done to our relationship with **God**.

1 John 4:10 MSG

Dear friends,
since **God**
so **loved** us,
we also ought
to **love** one another.

1 John 4:11 NIV

No man has at any time [yet] seen **God**. But if we **love** one another, **God** abides (lives and remains) in us and **His** **love** (that **love** which is essentially **His**) is brought to completion (to its full maturity, runs its full course, is perfected) **in us!**

1 John 4:12 AMPC

So we have come to know and to believe the **love** that **God** has for us. **God** is **love**, and whoever abides in **love** abides in **God**, and **God** abides in **him**.

What if I could speak
all languages of
humans and of angels?
If I did not **love** others,
I would be nothing more
than a noisy gong
or a clanging cymbal.

What if I could prophesy and understand all secrets and all knowledge? And what if I had faith that moved mountains? I would be nothing, unless I **loved** others.

1 Corinthians 13:2 CEV

What if I gave away
all that I owned
and let myself
be burned alive?
I would gain nothing,
unless I **loved** others.

1 Corinthians 13:3 CEV

Love is kind and patient,
never jealous, boastful,
proud, or rude.
Love isn't selfish
or quick tempered.
It doesn't keep a record
of wrongs that others do.

1 Corinthians 13:4–5 CEV

Love rejoices in the truth, but not in evil.

Love is
always
 supportive,
loyal,
hopeful,
and trusting.

1 Corinthians 13:7 CEV

1 Corinthians 13:8 CEV

So now
faith, hope,
and **love** abide,
these three;
but the greatest
of these is **love**.

1 Corinthians 13:13 ESV

His **love** endures forever.

Psalm 136:16 NIV

Now may
our **Lord** Jesus
(the Anointed One Himself)
and **God** our **Father**
(who has **loved** us, comforted us
eternally, and given us
a good hope by **His** grace)

bring comfort
to your hearts
and strengthen
your wills
to accomplish
every good work
and word.